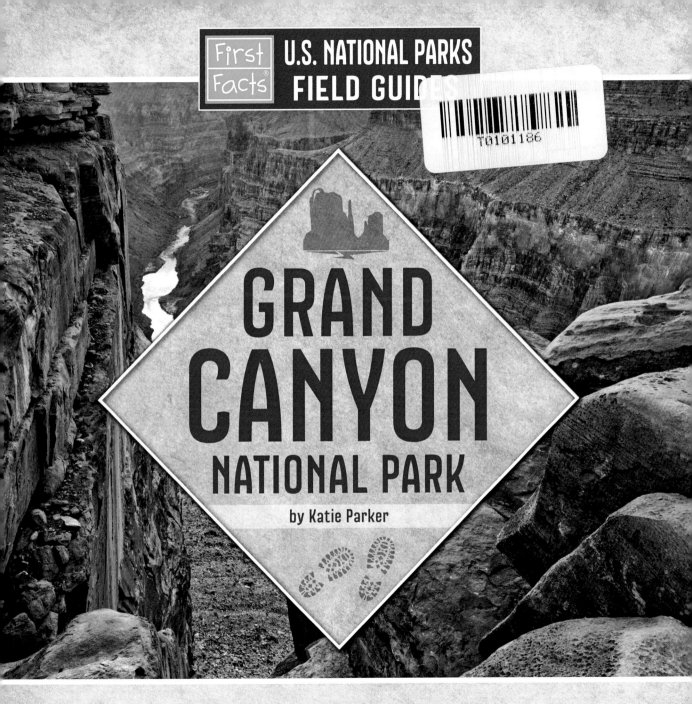

First
Facts®

U.S. NATIONAL PARKS
FIELD GUIDES

GRAND
CANYON
NATIONAL PARK

by Katie Parker

PEBBLE
a capstone imprint

First Facts Books are published by Pebble,
1710 Roe Crest Drive, North Mankato, Minnesota 56003
www.mycapstone.com

Library of Congress Cataloging-in-Publication Data is available
on the Library of Congress website.
ISBN 978-1-9771-0353-6 (library binding)
ISBN 978-1-9771-0523-3 (paperback)
ISBN 978-1-9771-0360-4 (ebook pdf)

Editorial Credits:
Anna Butzer, editor
Juliette Peters, designer
Tracy Cummins, media researcher
Kathy McColley, production specialist

Photo Credits:
Capstone: Eric Gohl, 9 Top, 13 Bottom, 17 Bottom; iStockphoto:
Anton Foltin, 1, benedek, Cover Bottom Middle; Newscom: Robert E.
Barber Stock Connection USA, 19 Inset; Shutterstock: Anton Foltin,
11, Bob Hilscher, 17 Top, Bram Reusen, 9 Bottom, Budimir Jevtic,
18 Right, Cat_arch_angel, Design Element, Christine Krahl, Design
Element, David G Hayes, Cover Bottom Left, Erik Harrison, 22–23,
24, Felicia Canfield, 15, Fredlyfish4, 13 Top, Galyna Andrushko,
Back Cover, Cover Top, ibrandify gallery, Design Element, James
Marvin Phelps, Cover Bottom Right, John D Sirlin, 6 Bottom, John
Sartin, 3 Bottom, Josemaria Toscano, 8–9, KanitHan, 3 Middle,
Kiril Kirkov, 18 Left, 19, Mike Chan, 2–3, Natalia Bratslavsky,
3 Top, NottomanV1, Design Element, Rex Wholster, 5 Bottom,
Roman Khomlyak, 20–21, RonGreer.Com, 6–7, Serj Malomuzh, 14,
Sharon Day, 12, sumikophoto, 5 Top, Thomas Trompeter, 20, Tom
Runge, 10, Vaclav Sebek, 18 Middle, viewgene, Design Element,
Wildnerdpix, 16–17

Printed and bound in the USA.
1335

Table of Contents

Welcome to the Grand Canyon......4

The South Rim.....................8

The North Rim....................12

The West Rim.....................16

Park Animals.....................18

Where to Stay....................20

Glossary 22

Read More 23

Internet Sites 23

Critical Thinking Questions....... 24

Index 24

Welcome to the Grand Canyon

Where can you see one of the most famous natural wonders of the world? Visit the Grand Canyon National Park! The Grand Canyon was formed almost six million years ago. The Colorado River **eroded** rock as it flowed through what is now Arizona.

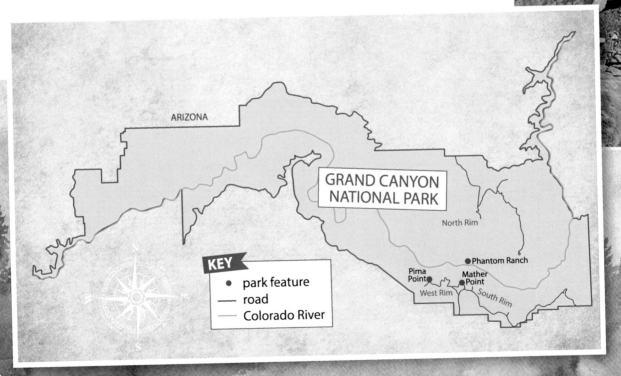

ARIZONA

GRAND CANYON NATIONAL PARK

North Rim

Phantom Ranch

Pima Point

Mather Point

West Rim

South Rim

KEY
- • park feature
- — road
- — Colorado River

FACT: How deep is the Grand Canyon? You could stack four Empire State Buildings on the canyon floor and just about reach the top of the canyon.

erode—to wear away

Grand Canyon National Park has more than 358 miles (576 kilometers) of trails to explore. The weather in the park depends on where you are. The **elevation** changes from the bottom of the canyon to the highest point on the rim or upper edge. There is a difference of 6,400 feet (1,950 meters). The temperature on the rim can be up to 20 degrees Fahrenheit warmer.

elevation—the height of the land above sea level

FACT: Visitors should dress in layers and bring plenty of water. Some parts of the park can reach 120°F (49°C) during the summer!

The South Rim

Many visitors begin their journey at the park's South Rim. Hike half a mile (0.8 km) from the Grand Canyon Visitor Center to Mather Point. Many people call the view from Mather Point the "true Grand Canyon." Visitors can see the Colorado River below and the layers of rock that make up the canyon.

view from Mather Point ∧

Yavapai Point

South Rim

South Entrance Road

Mather Point

KEY

- park feature
- visitor center
— Rim Trail
— trail
— road
canyon

FACT: Yavapai Point is the most northern point on the South Rim. The Yavapai Museum of Geology is located here. Visitors to the museum learn how the Grand Canyon formed.

∧ Kaibab Suspension Bridge

Visitors hike 6 miles (9.6 km) on the South Kaibab Trail to the Kaibab **Suspension Bridge**. This bridge passes over the Colorado River. Stop along the South Kaibab Trail to view the canyon. Popular spots are Ooh Aah Point, Cedar Ridge, and The Tipoff.

suspension bridge—a bridge hung from cables or chains strung from towers or mountains

mineral—a material found in nature that is not an animal or a plant

FACT: How did the Grand Canyon get its colors? Long ago, seas covered the land. As the water dried up, layers of **minerals** hardened into colorful rock.

∧ South Kaibab Trail

11

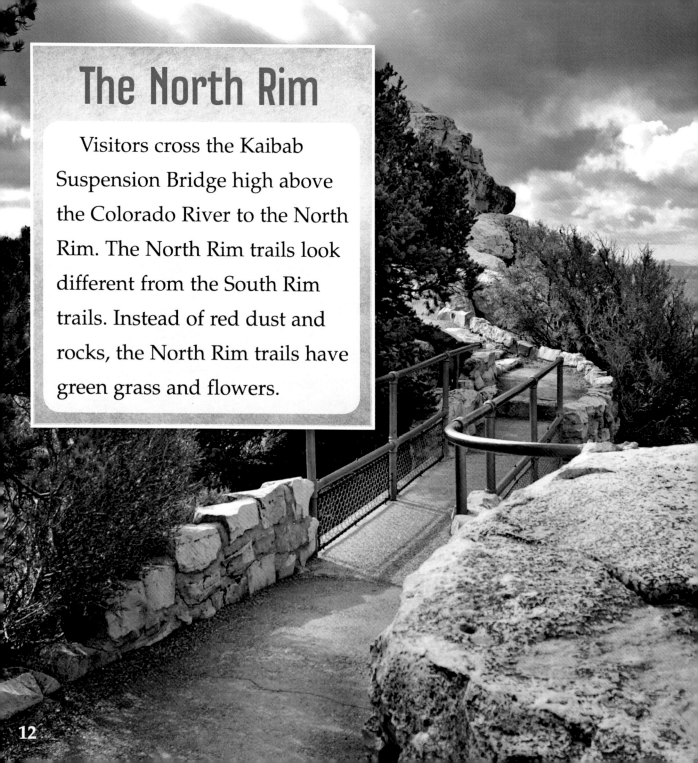

The North Rim

Visitors cross the Kaibab Suspension Bridge high above the Colorado River to the North Rim. The North Rim trails look different from the South Rim trails. Instead of red dust and rocks, the North Rim trails have green grass and flowers.

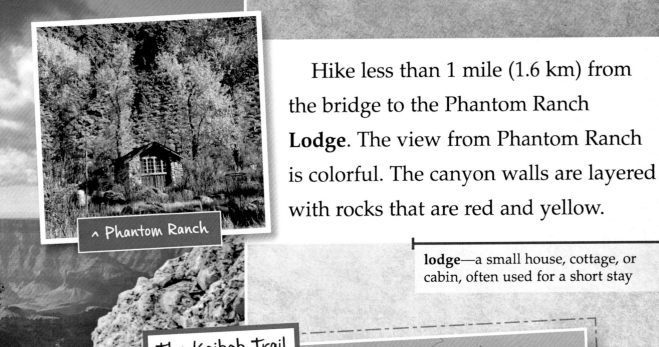

Hike less than 1 mile (1.6 km) from the bridge to the Phantom Ranch **Lodge**. The view from Phantom Ranch is colorful. The canyon walls are layered with rocks that are red and yellow.

^ Phantom Ranch

lodge—a small house, cottage, or cabin, often used for a short stay

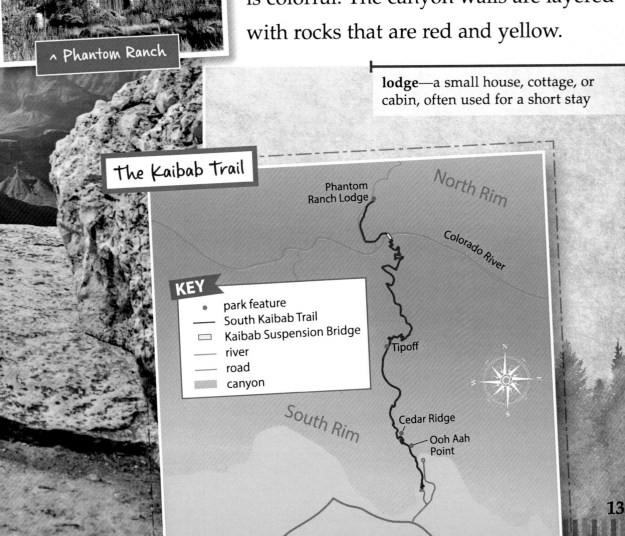

The Kaibab Trail

North Rim

Phantom Ranch Lodge

Colorado River

KEY
- • park feature
- —— South Kaibab Trail
- ▭ Kaibab Suspension Bridge
- —— river
- —— road
- ▨ canyon

Tipoff

South Rim

Cedar Ridge

Ooh Aah Point

13

The North Rim is about 1,000 feet (305 m) higher in **altitude** than the South Rim. It is also about 10°F cooler. The North Rim often gets 10 inches (25 cm) more of rain per year than the South Rim. Trees such as aspen, birch, maple, and oak are seen only on the North Rim. These trees need a lot of rainfall.

altitude—how high a place is above sea level or Earth's surface

FACT: Trails on the North Rim are closed from October to May because of snow.

The West Rim

Travel to the West Rim of the park to visit Mohave Point. From there you can see **vertical** cliffs that drop 3,000 feet (914 m). Visitors can hike 4 miles (6 km) west along the West Rim Trail to Pima Point. Looking east over the canyon, you can see 40 miles (64 km) into the distance.

∧ "The Battleship" rock formation which can be seen from Mohave Point

vertical—straight up and down

The West Rim

KEY
- park feature
- West Rim Trail
- trail
- road
- canyon

Pima Point

Mohave Point

West Rim

Park Animals

Grand Canyon National Park visitors see more than just rocks. As many as 500 kinds of animals live there. Bighorn sheep climb on the rocky canyon walls. Mountain lions, mule deer, and elk also live in the park. Gila monsters and chuckwalla lizards call the park home too. They are the two largest lizards in the United States.

^ mule deer

^ gila monster

^ chuckwalla lizard

^ bighorn sheep

FACT: Abert's squirrel, also called the tassel-eared squirrel, only lives in the Grand Canyon. It is the most common animal seen in the park.

Where to Stay

Hiking in the Grand Canyon can be hard work. But there are many places for visitors to rest and spend the night. The Grand Canyon Village on the South Rim has six lodges. On the North Rim, people often stay at Phantom Ranch. The ranch offers mule rides. Visitors can experience the sights of the Grand Canyon from the back of a mule.

∧ a lodge in Grand Canyon Village

Glossary

altitude (AL-ti-tood)—how high a place is above sea level or Earth's surface

elevation (e-luh-VAY-shuhn)—the height of the land above sea level

erode (i-ROHD)—to wear away

lodge (LOJ)—a small house, cottage, or cabin, often used for a short stay

mineral (MIN-ur-uhl)—a material found in nature that is not an animal or a plant

suspension bridge (suh-SPE-shuhn BRIJ)—a bridge hung from cables or chains strung from towers or mountains

vertical (VUR-tuh-kuhl)—straight up and down

Read More

Chin, Jason: *Grand Canyon.* New York: Roaring Brook Press, 2017.

Gregory, Josh: *Grand Canyon.* A True Book: National Parks. New York: Children's Press, an imprint of Scholastic, 2018

McHugh, Erin: *National Parks: A Kid's Guide to America's Parks, Monuments and Landmarks.* Revised edition. New York: Black Dog & Leventhal, 2019.

Internet Sites

Use FactHound to find Internet sites related to this book:

Visit *www.facthound.com*

Just type in 9781977103536 and go.

Super-cool stuff! Check out projects, games and lots more at **www.capstonekids.com**

Critical Thinking Questions

1. What items should you bring when you're going for a day hike in Grand Canyon?

2. Why are some plants and animals found only in certain areas of the park?

Index

animals, 18, 20

cliffs, 16
Colorado River, 4, 8, 10, 12

erosion, 4

Mather Point, 8
Mohave Point, 16

Phantom Ranch Lodge, 13, 20
Pima Point, 16

suspension bridge, 10, 12, 13

trails, 6, 10, 12, 16
trees, 14

Visitor Center, 8

weather, 6, 14